This Book Belongs to:

_____

This book features fun, new words to the song.

Louis Weber, C.E.O.
Publications International, Ltd.
7373 North Cicero Avenue
Lincolnwood, Illinois 60646

Permission is never granted for commercial purposes.

Manufactured in USA.

ISBN: 0-7853-0403-7

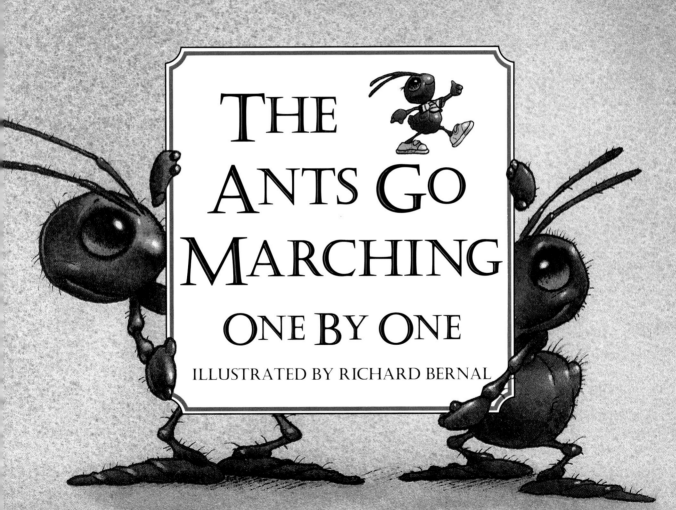

THE ANTS GO MARCHING

ONE BY ONE

ILLUSTRATED BY RICHARD BERNAL

Publications International, Ltd.

The ants go marching one by one.
　　Hurrah, hurrah!
The ants go marching one by one.
　　Hurrah, hurrah!
The ants go marching one by one;
　　The little one stops to suck his thumb,
And they all go marching down to the ground
　　To get out of the rain.

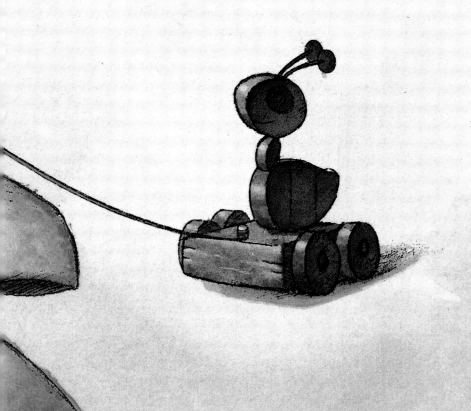

The ants go marching two by two.
    Hurrah, hurrah!
The ants go marching two by two.
    Hurrah, hurrah!
The ants go marching two by two;
    The little one stops to cry boo-hoo,
And they all go marching down to the ground
    To get out of the rain.

The ants go marching three by three.
　　Hurrah, hurrah!
The ants go marching three by three.
　　Hurrah, hurrah!
The ants go marching three by three;
　　The little one stops to ride a bee,
And they all go marching down to the ground
　　To get out of the rain.

The ants go marching four by four.
   Hurrah, hurrah!
The ants go marching four by four.
   Hurrah, hurrah!
The ants go marching four by four;
   The little one stops to ask for more,
And they all go marching down to the ground
   To get out of the rain.

The ants go marching five by five.
    Hurrah, hurrah!
The ants go marching five by five.
    Hurrah, hurrah!
The ants go marching five by five;
    The little one stops to jump and dive,
And they all go marching down to the ground
    To get out of the rain.

The ants go marching six by six.
   Hurrah, hurrah!
The ants go marching six by six.
   Hurrah, hurrah!
The ants go marching six by six;
   The little one stops to pick up sticks,
And they all go marching down to the ground
   To get out of the rain.

The ants go marching seven by seven.
   Hurrah, hurrah!
The ants go marching seven by seven.
   Hurrah, hurrah!
The ants go marching seven by seven;
   The little one stops to write with a pen,
And they all go marching down to the ground
   To get out of the rain.

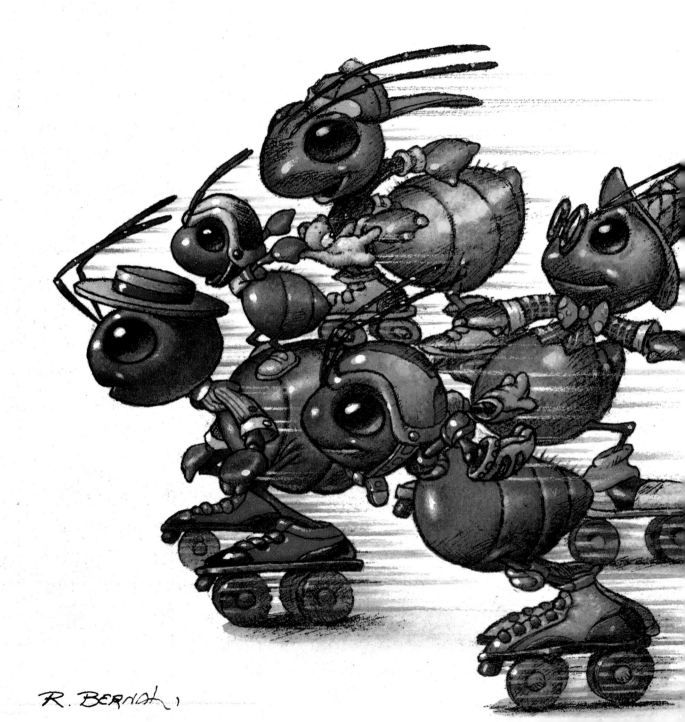

R. BERNAL

The ants go marching eight by eight.
    Hurrah, hurrah!
The ants go marching eight by eight.
    Hurrah, hurrah!
The ants go marching eight by eight;
    The little one stops to roller-skate,
And they all go marching down to the ground
    To get out of the rain.

The ants go marching nine by nine.
    Hurrah, hurrah!
The ants go marching nine by nine.
    Hurrah, hurrah!
The ants go marching nine by nine;
    The little one stops to drink and dine,
And they all go marching down to the ground
    To get out of the rain.

The ants go marching ten by ten.
    Hurrah, hurrah!
The ants go marching ten by ten.
    Hurrah, hurrah!
The ants go marching ten by ten;
    The little one stops to shout,
                    "THE END."